Brazil

Brazil

A Guide for Businesspeople

Jacqueline Oliveira

INTERCULTURAL PRESS

First published by Intercultural Press. For information contact:

Intercultural Press, Inc.
PO Box 700
Yarmouth, ME 04096 USA
207-846-5168
Fax: 207-846-5181
www.interculturalpress.com

Nicholas Brealey Publishing
36 John Street
London WC1N 2AT, UK
44-207-430-0224
Fax: 44-207-404-8311
www.nbrealey-books.com

© 2001 by Jacqueline Oliveira

Book and cover design and production: Patty J. Topel

All rights reserved. No part of this publication may be reproduced in any manner whatsoever without written permission from the publisher, except in the case of brief quotations embodied in critical articles or reviews.

Printed in the United States of America

05 04 03 02 01   1 2 3 4 5

Library of Congress Cataloging-in-Publication Data

Jacqueline Oliveira
   Brazil: a guide for businesspeople / Jacqueline Oliveira.
   p.   cm.
   Includes bibliographical references (p.   ).
   ISBN 1-877864-83-8 (alk. paper)
      1. Business etiquette—Brazil—Handbooks, manuals, etc.   2. Negotiation in business—Brazil—Handbooks, manuals, etc.   3. Corporations, American—Brazil—Management—Handbooks, manuals, etc.   4. National characteristics, Brazilian.   I. Title.

HF5389.3.B7 O38 2001
395.5'2'098—dc21   00-050594

Dedication

To Marian and Ruben, for your support, friendship, and this great opportunity; and of course, to Joe and Annique, *always*.

Table of Contents

List of Figures ix

Foreword xi

**Section One: Assumptions, Values,
Beliefs, and Attitudes** 1

   Collectivism 2

   Power Distance 5

   Masculinity/Femininity 8

   High Context/Low Context 12

   Hierarchy and Status 17

   Family 20

   Use of Time: Polychronic/Monochronic 23

   Dialogue-Oriented versus Data-Oriented 29

Section Two: Communication 33

   Verbal Communication 33

   Nonverbal Communication 36

   Relationships 44

Section Three: Business 53
  General Business Practices 53
  Managing in a Brazilian Workplace 62

Section Four: Protocol 71
  The Art of Eating 71
  Gift Giving 74
  Styles of Dress 75

Section Five: Information about Brazil 77
  Brazilian History, in Brief 77
  Map of Brazil 81
  The Country 82
  Race in Brazilian Culture 89

Bibliography 91

List of Figures

Figure 1
Brazil and other countries: Relative relationship on the Collectivistic/Individualistic scale 4

Figure 2
Brazil and other countries: Relative relationship on the Strong/Weak Power Distance scale 7

Figure 3
Brazil and other countries: Relative relationship on the Masculine/Feminine scale 11

Figure 4
Brazil and other countries: Relative relationship on the High-Context/Low-Context scale 16

Figure 5
Brazil and other countries: Relative relationship on the Polychronic/Monochronic scale 27

Figure 6
Brazil and other countries: Relative relationship on the Dialogue-Oriented/Data-Oriented scale 32

Foreword

Welcome to the intriguing world of Brazil. Our goal is to provide you with ample information about the Brazilian culture so that you will feel comfortable interacting with your Brazilian co-workers or business counterparts.

This manual contains information about Brazil—the country and the culture. Included are history, language, cognitive styles, culture qualities, social and workplace relationships, business negotiations, and miscellaneous information to help make your stay productive, interesting, and enjoyable. We hope that you will use this manual as a reference guide for many years.

Note that many of the cultural or sociological theories discussed in Sections One, Two, and Three are followed by suggestions that offer some applications of the information contained in the discussion. It is important that you, the negotiator or manager, understand both theory and application: theory for the why and application for the how. This way, you will be able to determine how to interact with a Brazilian counterpart in any business or organizational situation.

Throughout this manual *American* is used to refer to people from the United States of America. This term is used as a matter of convenience only, since *American* actually refers to all people from North and South America.

❈ *Section One* ❈

Assumptions, Values, Beliefs, and Attitudes

Assumptions, values, beliefs, and attitudes are the motivators by which a society forms its system of rules of behavior. This system comes about from the beginning of a culture's history and is formed by the intermingling of various cultural groups, geographic challenges, religious traditions, interactions with allies and enemies, and so forth. This system is comparable with the way that personal experiences and the environment mold an individual to behave in a certain way.

As a negotiator or manager, understanding these motivators is critical to knowing how to approach your international counterparts so that they will "hear" what you are saying.

The terms *collectivism, power distance,* and *masculinity/femininity* are based on the research of Geert Hofstede (1980, 42–63). The terms *high context/low context* and *polychronic/monochronic* are based on the research of Edward T. Hall (1981). The section on *dialogue-oriented* and *data-oriented* cultures is based on the research of Richard Lewis (1999).

Collectivism

> ***Collectivism*** **means the needs of the collective (i.e., the ingroups that people belong to such as family, church, employing organizations, etc.) are primary and the needs of the individual are secondary. This is opposite to the American's sometimes fierce devotion to individualism, which subjugates the needs of the collective to the needs of the individual (Hofstede 1980).**

- Brazil rates medium-high in terms of collectivism, along with Turkey and Iran; the United States rates extremely high in terms of individualism, along with Australia and Great Britain (see Figure 1).
- When one group member in a collective is criticized, the criticism reflects on the whole group.
- An example of Brazilian collectivism is the fact that personal and work lives are integrated; it is not unusual for large companies to help individual employees with personal financial problems; consequently, Brazilians tend to be very loyal to their employer (Adler 1997). This is very different from the U.S. work ethic in which the company is viewed as separate from the employee's personal needs; consequently, Americans tend to be less loyal to their employers.

Collectivism—Suggestions for the Negotiator

- Focus your presentations on the collective (as in "This is how your company, department, etc. will profit from this deal"), not on the individual (as in "This is what this deal will do for you").

- Because this collectivist norm is so prevalent in the Brazilian culture, many discussions about a potential project are important before decisions are made, since the decision will affect the group; consequently, decisions are not made quickly (more on this topic in "Making Decisions," pages 54–55).

- Be prepared to spend a lot of time discussing feelings about the ways the project will affect the company and the community.

Collectivism—Suggestions for the Manager

- Make an effort to periodically acknowledge the importance of the group to the success of the company.

- A helpful way to "take the pulse" of the staff is by keeping in touch with employee ingroups—knowing who is doing what; scores of games they might have recently played in; happenings in the family, such as visiting relatives, birth of a new baby, and so on.

- If you must criticize a member of your staff, do so privately (people in collectivist cultures "prefer that you talk 'in his back' and preserve his face"); remember that by criticizing the individual, you criticize the collective.

Figure 1:
Brazil and other countries: Relative relationship on the Collectivistic/Individualistic scale (Hofstede)

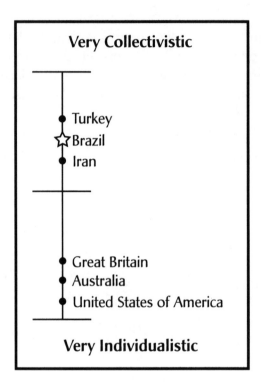

Power Distance

> *Power distance* means that authority is concentrated in the hands of a few, rather than distributed equally throughout society. It also means that people are less likely to question authority when it is concentrated in the hands of a few (Hofstede).

- Brazil rates medium-high on the power distance scale, along with Colombia and Chile; the United States rates medium-low, along with Canada and the Netherlands (see Figure 2).

- Managers from weaker power distance cultures (such as the United States) have some difficulty managing people from stronger power distance cultures (such as Brazil). The former manage by gaining approval through involving the group in decisions that will affect them. The latter manage by authority and do not include the group when making decisions or managing. Consequently, if an American manager in Brazil tries to involve subordinates in the management process, the Brazilian can become confused and perhaps even lose respect for the manager.

- An example of the stronger power distance norm in Brazilian workplace culture is the fact that businesses and other organizations tend to be hierarchical, in which lines of communication run more vertically than horizontally; in the United States, where power distance is relatively weak, lines of communication tend to run more horizontally than vertically.

Power Distance—Suggestions for the Negotiator

- Always address your Brazilian counterpart formally, using the title *Sénhor* or *Sénhora* plus the family name, unless and until your Brazilian counterpart suggests the use of first names. Your Brazilian counterpart may introduce himself or herself as Sénhor or Sénhora (first name), in which case respond in kind by introducing yourself as Sénhor/Sénhora (first name). (See "Titles," page 85.)

Power Distance—Suggestions for the Manager

- Always be friendly, but remember that inequality is expected in higher power distance cultures. Do not try to be "part of the team," as a manager would in the United States.

- You are expected to take a parental role as the manager of your organization. This means taking an interest in the well-being of your subordinates. For example, you would visit your employee or his or her relative who is in the hospital.

Figure 2: Brazil and other countries: Relative relationship on the Strong/Weak Power Distance scale (Hofstede)

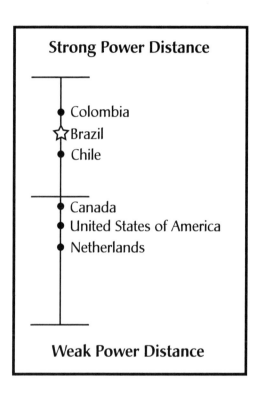

Masculinity/Femininity

> *Masculinity* as a cultural dimension means the degree to which the dominant values of a society are "masculine," demonstrating assertiveness and the acquisition of money and things (while not caring for others). *Femininity* in this context means the degree to which the dominant values of a society are "feminine," demonstrating affection, compassion, the ability and willingness to nurture, and emotionality (Hofstede).

- This index is not a reflection of machismo, which is male domination in a society, although machismo is a component of Brazilian society (more on machismo on pages 49–50); instead, it is a way of measuring the degree to which men in a society are comfortable nurturing others and displaying affection and emotion.

- Brazil rates medium (in the middle) on the masculinity/femininity scale, along with Israel and France (this is quite different from Brazil's Latin American neighbors, Venezuela and Colombia, which rate higher in terms of masculinity); the United States rates medium-high toward masculinity, along with Great Britain, Germany, and India. Sweden, on the other hand, rates quite high on the femininity scale (see Figure 3).

- This central location on the scale means that close relationships with friends, family, and colleagues are equally important to Brazilians (both men and women), as are making money and having symbols of success such as nice clothes, expensive automobiles, and nice apartments and homes.

Masculinity/Femininity—Suggestions for the Negotiator

- Brazilians rate a person's success by both family ties and success symbols, so be open to sharing information (that you are proud of) about your family. For example, the fact that a person's son is the CEO of a large company in Brazil suggests that the parents have done a good job at parenting (i.e., successful child equals good parenting). The parents are then afforded a certain degree of importance within the community by virtue of their family connection with their son. Equally, a person owning a luxury car suggests that this person has been successful in his or her work and/or investment dealings (or that a successful son is taking good care of his parents!).

- Always bear in mind the Brazilians' balance of masculine and feminine priorities. Do not be overly assertive or aggressive about getting down to business—this is looked upon by the Brazilians as arrogance and a sign of confused priorities.

Masculinity/Femininity—Suggestions for the Manager

- The feminine and collective norms of Brazilian culture mean that relations and friends are often hired by employers, regardless of skills and experience (the employers are taking care of their family and friends). Be prepared to work with extended family members, and remember that the relationship you establish with an employee in one department may affect your relationship with another in a different department. Consequently, it is best not to embarrass, publicly criticize, or in any way undermine any of your Brazilian employees or co-workers.

- To complete your projects successfully, focus both on the needs of the group, such as a comfortable work environment, good relationships between co-workers, periodic social gatherings for the employees and their families, and so forth (feminine), and on the rewards (masculine) that will be received upon a timely and successful completion of projects, such as salary increases, dinners at an expensive restaurant, or bonuses or other monetary awards (these, of course, must be in accordance with the corporate culture).

> *"You can always build skills but you can't alter the chemistry."*
> —*South American Manager*

Figure 3: Brazil and other countries: Relative relationship on the Masculine/Feminine scale (Hofstede)

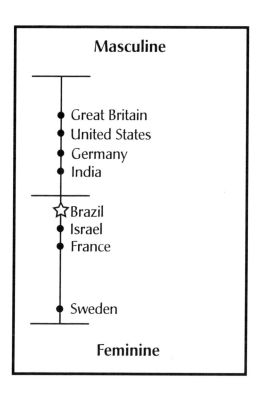

High Context/Low Context

> *Context* means to give meaning to a word or phrase or situation. It is a complex and deep value that is influenced greatly by cultural perceptions. In terms of cultural theory, there are two types of context: high context and low context. High-context cultures tend to find hidden or deep meaning in a word or phrase or situation by considering not only the spoken word, but other outlying influences, such as status or age of the people involved, physical environment, and body language—*your words say this, but your eyes say something else.* Low-context cultures tend to focus on the literal definition of a word or phrase, or the literal circumstances of a situation. These cultures do not rely on outlying influences to decipher a message and instead take the message at face value—*this is what you said, so this is what you mean* (Hall 1981).

- Hall, an American social scientist, conducted landmark studies about the ways different cultures perceive and assimilate information. He used the terms *high context* and *low context* to describe the two perspectives. High context describes cultures that focus primarily on the context in which a message is being transacted and pay less attention to the specific meaning of the message. Low context describes cultures that pay attention to the words of a message.

- Let's use the example of two men standing together in a room, beginning a conversation. One person is wearing a hat, the other is not. The person without the hat is older and of high-ranking position in the Catholic church, say, an archbishop. The archbishop says to the other man, "Nice hat."

    Now, the low-context response of the other man might be to say "Thank you." He has taken the literal definition of the phrase "nice hat" to mean "He likes my hat." A high-context response of the man might be to think, Oh, he is telling me that I should not be wearing my hat—after all, one does not wear a hat indoors; or one should not wear a hat in front of a high-ranking archbishop; or is he being sarcastic—is my hat ugly? or I should not be wearing a hat in front of someone older. The high-context response to the phrase "nice hat" might be to take the hat off and say, "I'm sorry. I should not be wearing my hat in front of you."

    In terms of the high-context response, meaning was read into the context of the situation and was influenced by the rank, status, and age of the archbishop and by the physical environment (being indoors.) His response to the seemingly innocuous phrase, "nice hat," is very different from the low-context, "face value" response (Hall 1981).

- Brazil rates above the median on the context scale, as a fairly high-context culture, along with Spain and Italy; the United States rates below the median on the context scale, but it is surpassed by Norway, Denmark, Sweden, the Netherlands, and Germany—all extremely low-context countries (see Figure 4).

- Brazilians use many verbal and nonverbal cues in communication, such as touching, facial gazing, tone of voice, body posture, social status, family history, and social setting. In addition, high-context communication requires time, since trust, friendship, personal needs, difficulties, and a myriad of other influences must be considered in the mix.

- An example of high-context behavior in the Brazilian business culture is the preliminary socializing and setting a tone (discussing unrelated topics such as the weather or sports) before business-related discussion begins. During this time, the Brazilian businessperson is getting to know the counterpart in a higher context, accomplished by learning the counterpart's interests (establishing similarities), learning about family background (and its connections), observing mannerisms (an indication of status and upbringing), listening to tone of voice (how passionate the person is about certain subjects), and so forth.

High Context/Low Context—Suggestions for the Negotiator

- Expect your Brazilian counterpart to pay attention to more than your words when you are speaking; hence, your clothing, personal style, nonverbal cues (eye contact, posture, gestures), and job title plus other intangibles will all be read and may in fact be taken more seriously than what you actually say.

- Your Brazilian counterparts will expect you to read them in the same way.

- Remember, since Brazilians are very adept at reading nonverbal cues, if you are acting in a way that is unnatural to you, they will sense your discomfort and question your sincerity. To the extent that you are personally comfortable, however, you might want to add dimension to your communication style, using more nonverbal gestures and tonal changes in your voice.

High Context/Low Context—Suggestions for the Manager

- Expect Brazilian employees to be emotive and use a lot of gestures; they are from a passionate culture and approach most situations with verve.

- The Brazilian employee may mistake the American even-keel temperament (the office is not the place for emotional outbursts, according to the American norm) as disinterest or judgment, so share your opinions and feelings (to the extent you are comfortable) with your employees.

Figure 4: Brazil and other countries: Relative relationship on the High-Context/Low-Context scale (Hall 1981)

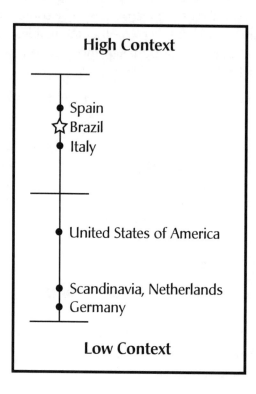

Hierarchy and Status

> Hierarchy and status are the manifestations of power distance in a society—how people react to authority when interacting with others. In Brazil, authority is respected by all and displayed (sometimes flaunted) by those who possess it.

- Society in Brazil is based on unequal relationships, with inequalities represented in financial status, family heritage, and ethnic origin.

- Status in business is based much more on *who* one knows as compared with *what* one knows.

- Status determines a lot in terms of professional interactions and negotiations. Initially, titles are used not so much as a means to identify the person's rank but to determine the comparative rankings of the others involved in the interaction. Secretaries are used a lot in the workplace to make or return calls, another symbol of the supervisor's authority, rank, and status.

- An example of hierarchy in the Brazilian culture is that Brazilians not only introduce themselves and others by title, they continue using titles for a longer time. Americans initially refer to themselves and others by title but prefer to quickly adjust to a first-name basis. Brazilians want to know how their rank compares with the person with whom they are speaking. They also want their rank to be known by others, when they are a high-ranking authority figure. (See more on this topic in "Titles," pages 34–35.)

- A reflection of status in Brazilian culture is the association with someone of a high rank within society, the company, or the community. It is not unusual to walk into a person's office or home and see a picture of that person with an authority figure. The picture may have been taken at a work-related function or a social function. The point is that the picture reflects that there has been contact with this authority figure and also suggests that there might be a tie or a relationship with that person.

Hierarchy and Status—Suggestions for the Negotiator

- Because of the emphasis on hierarchy, decisions are made at the top of the organizational management structure in Brazilian business; it is important for you to know the decision maker on the Brazilian team—your (and your team's) relationship with the decision maker is the barometer of negotiation success. Likewise, the Brazilians will expect your team to have a decision maker.

- Begin negotiations using titles and wait for your Brazilian counterpart to suggest a less formal atmosphere.

Hierarchy and Status—Suggestions for the Manager

- When you are assigning a project to your staff, Brazilian employees will first want to know who will manage and who will work on the project. This differs remarkably from the American tendency to approach a new project by outlining overall goals, designating major steps, and then (and only then) addressing staffing needs. Be sure to use the Brazilian approach, because relationships are critical to their commitment to a project.

- Because of the importance of hierarchy and status, Brazilians will be reluctant to bypass your authority if they disagree with you; however, this does *not* mean that they will be reticent about sharing their opinions with you or their peers. Be prepared for open conversations and the sharing of ideas, both with you and with peers (see "Dialogue-Oriented versus Data-Oriented," pages 29–32).

Family

For the Brazilian, the word *family* has a broad definition and encompasses blood relations, distant family, friends, and even colleagues at work. There is little distinction between family and the work environment. For the American, family is defined as blood relations. There is a distinction and a separateness between family and work.

The American tends not to divulge family concerns or intimate details at work. In fact many American companies do not allow family members to work together, either in the same department or sometimes even in the same company, for fear of nepotism—favoritism to family members. This way, the American is not or should not be preoccupied with family details in the workplace and can concentrate on the work at hand. The work environment is not the place to share intimate family matters.

The Brazilian, on the other hand, may work in the same company with family members, and goings-on in the home may carry over to the workplace. This is accepted and understood by peers and colleagues in the work environment.

- The family unit is the cornerstone of Brazilian society. Brazilians are rarely alone, and they do not understand the American need for alone time, thinking it a reflection that the individual does not have family or friends. Many young people stay at home after graduating from high school and move out of the home only if they are going abroad to college or university or getting married. The thought of American parents teaching their children to be independent so they can move out at age eighteen is perplexing to Brazilians.

- For the family-oriented Brazilian, family comes first, work comes second. This is a challenge for work-oriented Americans, many of whom focus on work before family or pleasure. It is not unusual for a Brazilian employee to forgo a work obligation if a family matter arises. Although the employer's reaction can be tumultuous—the employer may seethe and reprimand the employee soundly—for the most part, Brazilian co-workers and employers understand and acknowledge the employee's decision to put family first.

- Many extended family members and close friends live together in one Brazilian household.

- For the Brazilian, being from the right family and social class is of the utmost importance in terms of professional growth, whereas for Americans, education, experience, and hard work are the determining factors for professional growth and respect.

- Because families are so close to the Brazilian heart, discussions about personal details are reserved for the family and close friends, not acquaintances.

- Since the family unit is the cornerstone of life and revered in Brazilian culture, if you include Brazilian friends in a family occasion, such as inviting them to a family dinner, they will consider it a high honor.

Family—Suggestions for the Negotiator
- During your negotiations maintain good relationships with everyone on the team and counsel your team members to do the same. A perceived criticism or insult leveled at one person may be taken as an attack on any or all members of the team and/or on the extended family. Because of the need to protect relationships, a negative interaction or feeling may unduly jeopardize your negotiation.

Family—Suggestions for the Manager
- Be prepared to have brothers, sisters, in-laws, cousins, and close friends in the group that you manage.

- Employees may forgo a business obligation if a family matter arises. In such a case they may not come to work or fulfill their obligation. If this should occur, understand that family is paramount for the Brazilian. Consider building into your office policy a protocol that must be followed should a family matter arise that may affect office proceedings; for example, the employee must notify the supervisor or contact a previously approved colleague to take his or her duties.

- Brazilians will not usually take work home with them or want to accept telephone calls about work-related matters at home. Try not to call your colleagues or subordinates at home to discuss work matters unless they first offer their telephone number and suggest you call them at home.

- When engaging in pleasantries with your Brazilian counterparts, ask about the family, but do not ask personal questions unless your Brazilian counterpart has introduced the subject.

Use of Time: Polychronic/Monochronic

> From a cultural communication standpoint there are two different ways that cultures deal with the concept of time. One way views time as an undifferentiated whole within which many things happen at once. This view of time is called *polychronic*. In polychronic cultures, it is difficult to maintain schedules due to competing time commitments for other projects that require simultaneous attention. Interruptions and delays are a normal part of social and professional interaction.
>
> The opposite of *polychronic* is *monochronic*.* The monochronic view of time is linear—time unfolds "one thing at a time." In monochronic cultures, people tend to maintain tight schedules (Hall 1981).

- For the Brazilian, punctuality and adhering to schedules are not as important as human transactions, which means that a conversation will be finished, even if it means being late to another appointment.

- Because of the frequency of interruptions, meetings may go on for a long time.

---

* Richard D. Lewis, in *When Cultures Collide–Managing Successfully Across Cultures* (1996), uses the terms *multi-active* (polychronic) and *linear-active* (monochronic) to refer to time orientations.

- Brazil rates high on the polychronic (multi-active) scale, along with India and Pakistan; the United States rates high on the monochronic (linear-active) scale, along with Germany and Switzerland (see Figure 5).

- Professional men and women from the more industrialized cities of Brazil, such as Rio de Janeiro and São Paulo, are more likely than those from smaller cities to honor the monochronic view of time in their business dealings due to the influence of Europeans and North Americans; they may operate quite comfortably on American time or Swiss time.

Use of Time—Suggestions for the Negotiator

- Do not plan an ambitious agenda for a meeting—shorten your agenda (interruptions and late starts will throw you off schedule). Similarly, plan only one or two meetings in a day.

- Control your tendency to "cut to the quick" when beginning negotiations with your Brazilian counterpart; time is well spent discussing the theory of the proposed project and how it might affect the people involved.

- Expect to take several breaks.

- Expect to drink a lot of *cafezinho* (little coffee), which can be served as often as every two hours during several coffee breaks throughout the day.

- Expect meetings to begin late, with initial socializing. Once begun, expect them to run overtime.

- Be prepared to be involved in lots of conversation, both about the topic at hand and about totally unrelated matters.

- Expect frequent interruptions of your Brazilian counterpart's time, as she or he probably has several obligations to attend to at once, all of which are important.

- Double or triple the amount of time allotted for your negotiation proceedings, and do not be surprised if you must return to Brazil several times to complete your negotiations. Brazilians want to form relationships with the same people. If your company sends a different negotiating team for subsequent visits, the entire process of establishing relationships will have to begin again.
- A tactic used by some Brazilian businesspeople with American negotiators is stalling, sometimes forcing the time-conscious American to make concessions in order to maintain the schedule.

Use of Time—Suggestions for the Manager
- People in polychronic cultures like being busy; indeed, for both polychronic and monochronic cultures, the appearance of being busy is a reflection of being needed. Your Brazilian employees will thrive on having more than one project going at once. Being busy will afford them the opportunity to interface with several different project teams (relationship building) and show you, the manager, that they are multitask-oriented and capable of keeping many plates spinning. As the manager, your challenge is not to overwhelm them. You can begin your relationship with a particular employee by assigning one project, overseeing how he or she is handling it, then add another.
- Expect your Brazilian employees to spend time discussing projects that you have assigned them, that all-important relationship building, which is time-consuming but well worth it. If your employees feel they have good relationships with their peers, they will be more likely to want to work together and complete projects.
- When you assign projects, include more than an estimated time of completion—the time that signifies the completion of the project. Also include incremental time benchmarks for each phase of the project. The reason for this is two-

fold: first, you are honoring your American monochronic orientation by assigning time parameters to the project. Second, if the project falls behind schedule, you will notice this when incremental time benchmarks are missed and not be caught off guard when the final deadline is not met. You can then work with the employees to readjust incremental time benchmarks to either meet the deadline or change it.

Figure 5: Brazil and other countries: Relative relationship on the Polychronic/Monochronic scale (Hall 1983)

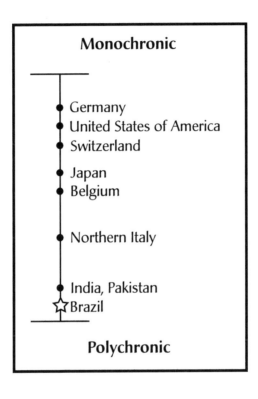

"American time" for a two-o'clock meeting
(ten minutes after two)

"Swiss time" for a two-o'clock meeting
(exactly two o'clock)

"Brazilian time" for a two-o'clock meeting
(thirty minutes after two)

Dialogue-Oriented versus Data-Oriented

> *Dialogue-oriented* cultures rely on *both* emotional data (feelings, intuition) and empirical data (facts and figures) in order to reach agreement and make decisions. In other words, they want to tap the office grapevine *and* analyze data. Only then do they believe they are well informed.
>
> The opposite of dialogue-oriented cultures are those that are *data-oriented*. These cultures rely primarily on research, analysis, facts, and figures to make decisions and reach agreement; they follow the adage "Numbers don't lie." Emotions are not to be trusted or even considered in the decision-making process (Lewis).

- Brazil rates very high on the dialogue-oriented scale, along with Italy, Spain, Portugal, and France. Not surprisingly, the United States rates high on the data-oriented scale, along with Germany, Switzerland, and New Zealand (see Figure 6).

- Through discussion, dialogue-oriented cultures process information and form conclusions. This is one of the reasons it is so important for Brazilians to share opinions and exchange information. This penchant for sharing opinions is done in an atmosphere of friendliness—not aggressively to prove each other wrong—and extends to everyone. For example, if an employee disagrees with an office policy, he or she will have no hesitation about discussing those feelings with peers, a supervisor, or friends.

- For Brazilians, the first priority is relationship building; the second priority is research and analysis. For Americans, the opposite is true: their first priority is research and analysis, and their second priority is relationship building.

- Brazilians want to talk about a proposed project before discussing the technicalities of research and analysis; Americans want to get right down to discussing the technicalities of research and analysis.

- Brazilians tend to get impatient with Americans who push facts and data as the sole component of a topic or project because they believe this is only part of the whole: feelings, issues, and opinions are equally important.

- The Brazilian will make every effort to avoid decisions that would negatively impact the family unit. If such a decision were absolutely necessary, steps would be taken to protect those family members who would be negatively affected by the decision. For example, in a situation in which a business decision may cause a family member to lose his or her job, a preliminary step (taken before the actual decision is put into effect) might be to transfer the family member to a different unit or department, thereby eliminating the possibility of his or her being laid off.

Dialogue versus Data—Suggestions for the Negotiator

- Expect to spend a great deal of time establishing good rapport with your Brazilian counterpart(s) through casual discussions and socializing. After good rapport is established, continue building the relationship(s) throughout the duration of the project. Although time-consuming, positive relationships will greatly enhance your chances of reaching an agreement in your favor.

- If at all possible, try to learn how people feel about your proposed project; in other words, try to become connected to the grapevine. This information may be helpful in understanding how to approach the Brazilian negotiating team. Also allow them time to gather impressions and opinions about the proposed project or issue.

Dialogue versus Data—Suggestions for the Manager

- Although you will be respected by virtue of the fact that you are the manager, in order to motivate your employees to work together to complete common goals, you must win them over. The American way of doing this is through rationality, facts, and data. This will not work in Brazil. Although facts and data are important to your Brazilian employees, equally important is how they view you as a manager and how confident they are that you are part of the group, thereby establishing your trustworthiness.

- When proposing something to your Brazilian employees, first discuss the benefit to the group, then support your position through empirical data.

Figure 6: Brazil and other countries: Relative relationship on the Dialogue-Oriented/Data-Oriented scale (Lewis)

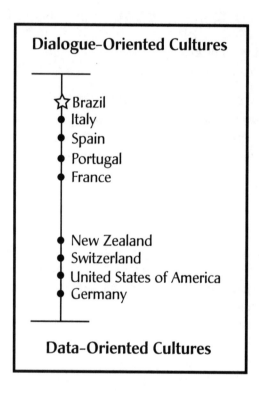

❈ *Section Two* ❈

Communication

Verbal Communication

Verbal and nonverbal communication are the exchange of information through speech and nonverbal language (body language) such as touching, rolling eyes, shrugging, facial gazing, gestures, hugging—and even the distance one stands from another (body orientation) during an interaction.

Brazilians express themselves with vigor both verbally and nonverbally; they feel uncomfortable with what they consider empty phrases, such as the American "Have a nice day!" or "How are you doing?" to which an honest response is neither expected nor desired.

Constant dialogue with few to no breaks is part of the Brazilian communication style. Many cultures, such as the American, use periods of silence to either emphasize or belabor a point in a conversation. For example, during contract negotiations, Americans average 3.5 silent periods of greater than ten seconds per thirty-minute sessions (Adler). These silent periods may be used either to manipulate or unbalance the position of the opponent or just as an opportunity to gather their thoughts before continuing. The Brazilians, on the other hand, average zero silent periods during a negotiation. Silence is just not part of the Brazilian repertoire when it comes to having a conversation.

In addition, Brazilian conversation style uses overlapping as a regular method of getting a point across. Overlapping is when more than one person is speaking at a given time. In the United States, when one person interrupts, the speaker usually stops talking and listens. Some cultures, such as the United States, consider overlapping to be rude or disrespectful. In contract negotiations, Brazilians interrupt, or overlap, each other more than twice as often as do American or Japanese negotiators (see boxed insert, page 38).

Language

- Portuguese is the official language in Brazil, although there are large pockets of Spanish-, Italian-, German-, and Japanese-speaking people in Rio de Janeiro and São Paulo. Pronunciation in Brazilian Portuguese is very different from continental Portuguese. The accents are much more nasal in tone.

- Many people feel that they can get away with speaking Spanish in Brazil (Brazil is the only South American country whose language is *not* Spanish). Although this is, to an extent, true—if Spanish is spoken slowly, the Brazilian counterpart will most likely be able to understand and respond—it is not always appreciated. Learn at least a few Portuguese pleasantries. It will serve you well as a guest in Brazil, showing respect and a willingness to learn.

Titles

- The standard for using titles has changed over the years. In the past, when constant formality was the norm, titles were used in the business relationship. Today, titles are not used as often, or they may be used with a first name.

- Brazilians retain two last names. When using a title, use the second last name with the title; in other words, Carlos Oliveira de Carvalho, a professor, is Professor Carvalho.

Conversation Topics: Dos and Don'ts

Americans may find that Brazilians are much more open about topics of conversation, initiating conversations that may be uncomfortable or embarrassing for the American. For instance, it is not unusual for a Brazilian to make mention of one's weight or skin disorders or other physical characteristics. Talking about salaries or the cost of an expensive item is acceptable in Brazil, but often not so in the United States, where such subjects are usually taboo. One explanation for this openness (especially about physical characteristics) is that the Brazilians feel that it is wise to acknowledge a possible point of embarrassment and then move beyond it in conversation (Harrison 1983).

Conversation Dos

- Soccer (*fútbol*) and other sports
- Foods, scenic spots, historical sights, customs, folk art, weather

Conversation Don'ts

- Politics
- Argentina (Brazil's traditional rival)
- Age
- Sex and obscene jokes
- Marital status
- Family, initially—this may be surprising, given that Brazilians are extremely family-oriented. However, family is a topic that is private and not to be shared in detail with an acquaintance. However, after the passage of time, and af–

ter acquaintance turns to friendship, asking about family members is acceptable, even expected.

- During conversation, do not refer to yourself as an "American"; refer to yourself either as a "North American" or "from the United States." Brazilians, along with citizens of all countries on the American continents, are also Americans and do not take kindly to what is seen as an ethnocentric value. In addition, do not refer to Brazilians as Latin Americans, Latinos, or Hispanics. Unlike its neighbors, Brazil is a former Portuguese colony, not a former Spanish colony. Also, as noted earlier, Brazilians do not take kindly to someone assuming they speak Spanish. They are very proud of their Portuguese heritage and may be offended if a foreigner speaks to them in Spanish.

Nonverbal Communication

Knowing what you are conveying through your body language and being able to interpret your Brazilian counterpart's body language is critical to the accurate exchange of information, not to mention relationship building.

Gestures

Brazilians have myriad gestures that they use profusely and with abandon, during both social and professional exchanges. Here are a few that you may come into contact with when working or socializing with Brazilians.

Attention Getting

- Pointing directly to one's mouth with the index finger and using a fluttering motion (the finger does not touch the lips): "I want to talk with you."

- Stretching the arm away from the body either vertically or at a 45-degree, upward angle, with palm open and facedown, while the fingers are flexed in a downward motion: "Come here."

Section Two

- Imitating holding a telephone to one's ear: "You have a phone call."
- A hissing sound, made by blowing through closed teeth and pursed lips, sounding like "psiu psiu": "Come here" (used in informal situations).

Departure
- Making a fist and opening it quickly: "Go away." This can also be used to indicate that you need to leave or that you would like a situation to go away. This is often a precursor to saying good-bye.

Miscellaneous Gestures
- *Figa*, a fist with the tip of the thumb protruding between the index and middle fingers: a gesture of good luck. (This gesture is considered rude and/or obscene in some other Latin countries and in most Mediterranean countries.)
- Punching a fist into the hand: a vulgar gesture.
- Snapping the fingers while whipping the hand up and down: used to emphasize a point.
- Brushing the fingertips under the chin: "I don't know."
- Pinching the earlobe: an expression of appreciation.
- *Cornudo*, index and little finger pointing upward (like horns) with the remaining fingers folded down: suggests infidelity.
- Gestures that suggest having coffee together:

    extending the little finger and thumb, while folding the middle fingers, pointing the thumb toward the mouth and simulating a drinking motion.

    extending the index finger and thumb parallel about two inches apart, with the remaining fingers folded.

touching the index finger to the thumb, while folding the remaining fingers, simulating a drinking motion.

An American gesture that is particularly offensive to the Brazilians: the OK sign (thumb and index finger making a circle with other fingers extended). This is a very vulgar gesture in Brazil. Use the thumbs-up sign instead.

> ### *Some Differences between American and Brazilian Communicative Behavior during Meetings*
>
> - **Silent periods**: numbers of silent periods greater than ten seconds: Americans–3.5, Brazilians–0
> - **Conversational overlaps**: more than one person speaking at a time per ten-minute period: Americans–10.3, Brazilians–28.6
> - **Facial gazing**: looking directly in the face of one's counterpart, per ten-minute period: Americans–3.3, Brazilians–5
> - **Touching** (not including handshakes): per ten-minute period: Americans–0, Brazilians–4.7 (Adler)

Proxemics (Space Considerations)
- The average distance that Americans maintain from one another in a public situation (walking down a crowded street, for instance) is 1-1/2 to 4 feet; this distance is about 1 to 3 feet for the Brazilian.

- Brazilians find the American tendency to say "excuse me" when bumping into people in a crowd to be overdoing politeness and may even consider it insincere—for the Brazilian, touching people, jostling, and bumping are a natural part of life and not something that one should apologize for.

- Brazilians tend to stand much closer than Americans do when engaged in conversation. Thus, the American tendency is to back away from the Brazilian, thereby maintaining distance, initiating a kind of dance: as the Brazilian moves forward, the American moves back. This backing away is considered rude to the Brazilian.

- Brazilian interactions involve more touching than do typical American interactions. In one study, Brazilians were observed to touch each other (not including handshakes) almost five times per thirty-minute period; in the same study, Americans touched zero times (Adler).

- Americans see touching as a sign of a very close relationship, sometimes intimacy.

- Brazilians tend to show affection through hugging (*abraço*), backslapping, kissing, and so forth. These gestures are not necessarily forms of intimacy but are gestures of friendliness and concern.

- Touching is particularly obvious during conversations among Brazilian men, who may emphasize a point by putting an arm around the person spoken to, or touching his arm or stomach. Men may also be seen walking arm in arm.

- Women in social situations tend to touch more than men during conversation, sometimes curling fingers around the other's hair, playing with buttons, stroking the arm of the partner, or when walking together, linking arms.

- Women tend not to touch as often in business situations, and rarely will they touch men.
- In business situations, the higher-ranking person usually initiates touching.

Proxemics—Suggestions for the Negotiator
- Touching is something that occurs between negotiators but rarely across the negotiating table while business is being conducted. Touching occurs between negotiations. For example, when exiting the room, the Brazilian businessperson may put his arm briefly about the shoulder of the American counterpart as they walk through the door. The same gesture may occur when the teams break for a meal and are in a restaurant.
- Expect to shake hands with everyone on the Brazilian team, both upon greeting and leave-taking.
- The American businesswoman may experience these friendly gestures from a Brazilian male counterpart but rarely from the female. Do not back away or view it as sexual harassment. Neither American men nor women should consider this to be an attempt at coercion on the part of the Brazilian. It is merely a gesture of openness.

Proxemics—Suggestions for the Manager
- Although touching occurs within the office environment, hierarchy and status determine who initiates the touching. Those of a higher rank can touch those of a lower rank, but not vice versa. Rarely will a Brazilian subordinate initiate touching by putting his or her arm around the boss. This would be viewed as lack of respect for authority. You may see the Brazilian authority figure putting his arm around the subordinate—this is viewed as the parent taking care of the family member.

- American managers who are comfortable touching may do so, but only a light gesture (hand briefly placed on the shoulder) and man to man. Steer clear of cross-gender touching. Even in the most open cultures (such as Brazil), gestures can still be misinterpreted. Instead, the female American manager can instill a feeling of openness through smiling, direct eye contact, shaking hands, and engaging in social conversations.
- Remember, your Brazilian employees view touching as a sign of concern. If you are not demonstrative in this way, they may interpret your demeanor as a sign of dislike or as a lack of trust.

Facial Gazing
- Facial gazing is the tendency to look directly at the face of one's counterpart, often known as direct eye contact.
- Brazilians tend to facial gaze much more than Americans do.
- Brazilians stand directly facing one another when engaged in conversation, which allows them to maintain direct eye contact.
- Americans tend to feel that the Brazilians are staring at them, sometimes viewing this as an intimidation tactic during business negotiations.
- For women, facial gazing can be particularly disconcerting because it can be perceived as containing sexual overtones.

Facial Gazing—Suggestions for the Negotiator
- Expect your Brazilian counterpart to make prolonged, direct eye contact with you throughout negotiation procedures. Try not to look away often or stare back intensely.

Facial Gazing—Suggestions for the Manager

- Your Brazilian employees may maintain prolonged, direct eye contact with you. This is a sign of respect for you as their leader; do not interpret it as aggressive behavior.

Greetings and Partings

- Handshakes are the usual greeting, although they tend to be less firm than those of Americans. Men shake hands often. Even when meeting small groups of people, they will shake hands with each person in the group. Men who know each other well may add a pat on the back or the stomach.

- If two people are merely acquainted, the greeting is usually a nod of the head and a smile. Sometimes a simple acknowledgment is used, such as *"Tchau,"* which is similar to the American "Hey!"[†]

- If two men know each other, they usually stop (even if late for an appointment), shake hands, and exchange pleasantries; women usually kiss and exchange pleasantries.

- If two people know each other rather well, sometimes the abraço is used with or without the handshake.

- Occasionally a Brazilian woman who feels that she knows a North American man well will draw him close to her and offer her cheek to be kissed; the proper response is to brush his cheek against the woman's and simulate a kiss.

[†] Pronounced like the Italian "ciao," it is also used in leave-taking.

Section Two

Greetings and Partings—Suggestions for the Negotiator
- Remember to shake the hand of all those in your group. The only time you would not shake the hands of group members is if the meeting is in a crowded restaurant and you would have to reach over the table, in which case you would acknowledge the individual through eye contact and a nod.

Greetings and Partings—Suggestions for the Manager
- Remember the importance of building and maintaining relationships with your Brazilian subordinates. Taking a moment to be friendly will take you far on the road to effective management. When you greet or leave a Brazilian subordinate, try to say something friendly, such as "Wasn't that a great fútbol game last night?" or "Crazy weather, eh?" If you are in a hurry, you may say something like "See you tomorrow" while you indicate that you must keep the interchange short. Even the most innocuous statement will be evidence that you are open to building a relationship with your team.

The Kiss

The kiss is used more often in Brazil than in the United States and is a gesture of intimacy and close friendship. Although it is used more frequently between women, it can occasionally be used between men in social situations.

The kiss between women is not really a kiss on the cheek, as it appears. The counterparts touch cheeks and kiss the air; sometimes, it is merely a swinging motion over the counterpart's shoulder. The kiss begins by touching right cheeks and can alternate between cheeks from two to five times.

"I know of a young American girl being 'hustled' by a Carioca boy, who insisted on kissing her passionately on a crowded rush-hour bus. She resisted, pointing out all the people watching them. His very Brazilian response: 'Close your eyes.'"

(Harrison, 23)

Miscellaneous Customs Particular to Brazil

- Waving at an acquaintance who is at a distance is acceptable, but do not shout at the person.

- When eating, do not touch the food with your hands; this includes eating a sandwich or a pizza, which is usually cut with a knife and fork; if hands must be used, hold the food with a napkin. Even fruit is eaten with a knife and fork (more on eating in "The Art of Eating," pages 71–74).

- Men may stare at women in a public place; women typically ignore this behavior.

- People do not walk down the street while eating or chewing gum, although eating ice cream or candy is acceptable. If you buy food at a *barzinho* (informal street café or bar), stand near the establishment to eat.

Relationships

Forming and building relationships refers to the factors that motivate a culture to form committed relationships. For the negotiator and manager, this means knowing what type of motivation workers in a culture need in order to commit to a project.

Social Relationships

Brazilians are extremely social; they enjoy being with friends and relatives and prefer a social forum to being alone. Brazilians are perplexed by the American need for alone time.

Even occasions that Americans may feel are staid, such as an official business meeting or a family get-together after a funeral service, are opportunities for social exchange for the Brazilian. Because Brazilians are so adept at social interchange, one would rarely find a Brazilian being inappropriate in any situation. The Brazilian shares conversation as a reflection of his or her concern and openness.

Depending on the needs of the individuals involved, American social relationships may hover at the acquaintance stage for a long time before (if ever) moving on to a deeper friendship. Brazilians tend to breeze through the acquaintance stage and move on to more familiar stages quickly. For example, the Brazilian is much more likely to get to know the daily postal deliverer personally than is the American, who may simply exchange pleasantries, then go on with business.

Business Relationships

First and foremost, building a strong relationship with all those with whom one does business is of primary importance to the Brazilian. Trust is the key to doing business in Brazil.
- Brazilian businesspeople maintain a friendly air throughout the negotiation process. This does not indicate a lackadaisical attitude toward business; on the contrary, Brazilian businesspeople are very savvy, strong negotiators. The friendly attitude is a way to establish trust in the potential foreign business partner.‡

---

‡ The Brazilian businessperson will want to establish a trusting relationship with each member of the team. Since this is time-consuming, maintain the same team members throughout the negotiation process.

- Only after a relationship and trust have been established will the Brazilian enter into serious negotiations. This process takes time, and the relationship must be continually nurtured throughout the life of the project.

- For the high-context Brazilian, the spoken word is more binding than the written word (a contract); this is the opposite of the American low-context tendency to rely on a written contract over the spoken word.

- For the Brazilian, the motivating factor in business is usually power and prestige, not necessarily money, as it normally is for the American.

- Americans, coming from a country where the legal system is pervasive and reliable, often enter into business relations with a stranger and maintain a strictly business relationship throughout the process, because retribution for dishonesty will be relatively swift and unprejudiced.

- In Brazil, the legal system is not as responsive to resolutions of justice as in the United States, due in part to corruption, bureaucratic red tape, and a lack of system infrastructure. Hence, Brazilians are not as litigious as Americans; they tend not to rely on the intervention of authorities in business or personal problems. Brazilians are reticent about entering into business deals with someone they do not know. If the counterpart proves untrustworthy, they may not be able to recoup their investment—hence, the importance of building relationships and trust. Brazilians assume that a friend will not be untrustworthy.

Business Relationships—Suggestions for the Negotiator
- If at all possible, make sure that your Brazilian counterpart has knowledge of you and your party before you arrive, if possible, via a business liaison (see boxed insert, page 48). The following should be communicated: (1) the purpose, nature, and potential benefits of your proposal;

Section Two

(2) background information about you and your colleagues; and (3) you and your colleagues' responsibilities.

- Learn a few phrases of Portuguese and use them during the introduction phase of your negotiations.

- Establishing a relationship and thereby trust takes a great deal of time and lots of socializing; this is accomplished through low-key interactions in restaurants and clubs and joining your counterpart at sporting or cultural events. By participating in social events such as these, you are showing your colleague(s) that you are committed to the relationship.

- Never believe that because you have a signed contract, the agreement is set in stone. Even after you have signed a contract, continue to build your relationship with your Brazilian counterpart to ensure that the project is carried through to completion.

Using an Interpreter

Many cross-cultural misunderstandings have occurred in business negotiations because the parties did not adequately understand the language and the culture. If your negotiations are to be conducted in English, determine before the initial meeting whether your counterpart has a working knowledge of English and understands the U.S. American culture. If the negotiations are to be conducted in Portuguese and you do not speak Portuguese fluently and are not familiar with the Brazilian culture, consider using an interpreter. Certified interpreters can be contracted through embassies and international organizations located in the United States.

Business Relationships—Suggestions for the Manager

- Establish a social relationship with your Brazilian employees by demonstrating an interest in their personal lives and by being willing to share some aspects of your personal life with them. You may consider occasionally hosting a lunch either in the office or at a restaurant, and join in with the group during coffee breaks.

> ### Establishing a Business Contact in Brazil
>
> A business contact (sometimes referred to as a liaison or intermediary) is a person or organization that provides initial contacts between the foreign businesspeople and Brazilian counterparts. Intermediaries are usually contracted before the initial visit by the foreign businessperson. These contacts are local Brazilian entities and are critical to the negotiation process. They provide letters of introduction, set up initial meetings, and establish contacts for the foreign businessperson. Some good business contacts in Brazil are local accounting firms, attorneys, business consultants, embassies, and the American Chamber of Commerce located in Brazil.

Business Relationships—Women

- Gender issues in this context refer to the way that women are treated differently from men in work and social environments.

- Many North American businesswomen have difficulties interacting with Brazilian businessmen due to the machismo attitude that is present in the culture. Some North American businessmen have difficulty conducting business with Brazilian men who treat women in their presence with a macho flair, whether or not the object of the flirtation is a Brazilian or an American woman.

- In the larger, more sophisticated cities, such as Rio de Janeiro and São Paulo, women (especially North American businesswomen) are more likely to be treated equally, or at least with an overlay of equality, than in less cosmopolitan cities. Brazilian men may, nonetheless, still behave in a chivalrous manner toward women.

- In the Brazilian social environment, men show their appreciation for women verbally and physically through catcalls, staring, compliments, and occasional touching. Brazilian women usually ignore these intrusions and carry on as if they have not heard or felt anything. This male attention should not be interpreted, necessarily, in the same negative light as it would back home.

Business Relationships, Women—Suggestions for the Negotiator

- Expect American businesswomen to be treated in a chivalrous manner by Brazilian men. Accept this attitude and continue with your work without drawing undue attention to this treatment.

- If you are out in public with your male Brazilian counterpart, he may make comments about women passing by or women in the restaurant you are in. Acknowledge the comment and continue with the subject at hand.

Business Relationships, Women—Suggestions for the Manager

- Expect a degree of machismo from your male Brazilian employees, and expect your female Brazilian employees to accept this attitude. Unless you sense that the macho attitude is becoming overbearing or that the female employee does not seem to be appreciating the overture, do not intervene—this is how genders interface in Brazil. If you feel that you need to intervene, take the employee(s) aside, individually and privately, and discuss your feelings, asking the male to tone down his behavior and the female to alert you if she feels pressured or upset by this individual. Should the problem persist, follow company protocol in dealing with conflicts between employees.

- If you also have American employees, expect some problems to result from the Brazilian machismo. One way to deal with this issue is to prepare your American employees by explaining this cultural norm and by explaining to your Brazilian employees that North Americans often find macho behavior offensive or disturbing. These conversations should be held in private, with employees of only one culture present, *never together.*

Being an American Businesswoman Working with Brazilians

Here are some tips for the American businesswoman working within the Brazilian culture (Leaptrott 1996).

- Do not enter your relationships with Brazilian counterparts feeling disadvantaged—you are not. Be yourself and be prepared for, and patient with, cultural differences.

- To the extent that time allows, become familiar with Brazilian cultural arts such as painting, literature, music, cuisine, and so on. Also learn about sports such as soccer and use this knowledge to introduce conversational topics that you can draw upon during your social engagements with the Brazilians. This will distract others from the fact that you are a woman and will put you and your counterparts more at ease.

Section Two

- Be available to socialize with Brazilian businesswomen, but do not gravitate only toward women. Instead, develop and maintain relationships with both male and female counterparts.
- Speak confidently, yet with a soft voice.
- The Brazilian handshake is firm, although less so than the typical American handshake. Return the handshake with the same degree of intensity of grip.
- Dress in sophisticated, fairly conservative suits and matching accessories. Personal image is important.
- Sometimes your presence as a woman may be a plus. Since women are trained to be more high context than men, you may be more likely to read between the lines during negotiations and be more sensitive to what is not said than your male counterparts.
- Do not offer to meet your Brazilian counterpart in a bar after work; suggest a restaurant instead.

A Note to American Men

It is sometimes difficult for American men to ignore the overt machismo of the Brazilian culture, especially when such behavior is not condoned by the American business culture. Be aware of this cultural attitude before you go to Brazil, and be sure that all of your business associates, male and female, are equally apprised. It would be unusual if your Brazilian counterpart's machismo spilled over to vulgar or offensive actions. Most likely, their actions originate from Brazilian chivalry.

If you are offended by an action, or if a female associate is offended, speak privately to a third party who will intervene on your behalf. Explain to the third party that you and your associates want very much to build a strong relationship with your Brazilian counterpart and that you wish to understand Brazilian cultural attitudes, but because women are treated differently in the United States, you find his actions toward the female contingent to be upsetting.

❊ *Section Three* ❊

Business

General Business Practices

Some Negotiation Tactics Used by Brazilians

- *"Stalling."* Taking extensive periods of time can look like stalling. This behavior may simply be the Brazilian time-consuming process of relationship building. Brazilians, however, are well acquainted with the American tendency to be impatient and have used stalling to get what they want by waiting until the end of the planned negotiation schedule to make a demand or push a position.

- *Bargaining.* Brazilians enjoy the bargaining process and may want to hash over details to a frustrating extent for the Americans present. The Brazilians may appear to concede grudgingly only after a long period of debate over a point.

- *Soft Sell.* Brazilians like the soft-sell approach to business, in which conversations cover not only the technicalities of the proposition but also the potential impact the proposed project will have on the people involved. Americans usually prefer the hard-sell approach in which facts and figures dominate and decisions are made based on numbers and other objective considerations, not on feelings (see "Dialogue-Oriented versus Data-Oriented," pages 29–32, for more detail).

- *Embellishing the Truth.* Brazilians may make a problem seem insurmountable (then, in time, be able to successfully solve the problem) in order to appear powerful. They may sometimes stretch the truth to their advantage and will expect their foreign counterparts to do the same.

- *Lack of Unity.* Brazilian negotiation team members may sometimes disagree with each other or try to outdo their teammates. But be careful: this may or *may not* be a negotiation tactic to confuse their foreign counterparts. Nonetheless, Brazilian negotiation teams sometimes genuinely lack unity—quite a different style from the American negotiation team that usually acts like a "well-oiled machine."

- *Prolonged, Direct Eye Contact.* When Brazilians make direct eye contact for long periods of time (see "Facial Gazing," pages 41–42), you may be tempted to interpret this as "staring" and thus as intimidating or manipulative.

Making Decisions

- Due to the strong hierarchical nature of Brazilian corporate structure, decisions are made "at the top" in Brazilian business culture (see "Hierarchy and Status," pages 17–19). This is different from the American norm in which decision making is spread throughout the organization.

- It is important to meet and get to know the highest-ranking person involved in the business or organization, since this will probably be the person who will make decisions.

- Decision making involves risk and is not something the Brazilian businessperson takes to aggressively. Most support employees or midlevel managers will be reluctant to make decisions in the workplace, specifically because they want to avoid risk. This can be frustrating for American managers in Brazil, who expect their midlevel managers to make decisions.

Making Decisions—Suggestions for the Negotiator
- Do not try to rush the decision-making process. It is time-consuming when dealing with Brazilians.

Making Decisions—Suggestions for the Manager
- Because of the Brazilian reluctance to take risks in the work environment, it may be difficult to obtain accurate progress reports from Brazilian employees—they may say "all is well" when in fact it is not. Two ways to deal with this issue are to

    maintain dialogue with your supervisor in order to keep abreast of progress, and

    reinforce that written reports are part of the American management style and something you require from your supervisees.

Meetings and Presentations
- Business meetings in Brazil usually start late, sometimes fifteen minutes to an hour after the appointed time.

- The atmosphere in a business meeting is usually informal and friendly; don't be misled by the style of dress—businesspeople usually keep their suit jackets on throughout the meeting.

- If business cards have not been exchanged previously, they are exchanged at the beginning of the first meeting.

- The first part of the meeting is taken up with casual conversation (lasting ten to fifteen minutes). Brazilians do not appreciate the American tendency to want to get down to business right away.
- Interruptions are frequent during meetings. Expect this, and be patient when meetings take much longer than expected.
- Meetings are usually held in offices or in restaurants or clubs, often over lunch. (Americans are sometimes surprised to find that alcohol is often served during lunch.) Business is not usually discussed during dinner, however.
- Frequent coffee breaks occur during meetings, sometimes as often as every two hours.
- Brazilians enjoy creativity and diversity in presentations; they like to be entertained.

Meetings and Presentations—Suggestions for the Negotiator

- Although meetings usually begin late, this does not mean that you should be late. Punctuality is important; you may want to bring work with you to do while you are waiting.
- Try to schedule meetings in your office (if you have an on-site office). This way you will be more in control of punctuality and interruptions; otherwise, schedule the meeting in your Brazilian counterpart's office—this venue is much better than a public environment, such as a restaurant or club, where you will be less able to avoid interruptions.
- Do not schedule more than one or two meetings in a day; the lack of punctuality will put you behind schedule, and you will be rushed.

Section Three

- Don't forget to begin all meetings with casual conversation. Do not rush into talking about the business at hand.

- Begin all presentations with a story to illustrate your point; use a multimedia approach with charts, graphs, mockups, and so on.

- Remember that Brazilians appreciate variety. They will not appreciate a set, inflexible agenda.

Meetings and Presentations—Suggestions for the Manager

- Schedule regular meetings with your staff. These meetings will fulfill a dual purpose: keeping you abreast of projects and socializing. Be sure to have refreshments available during the meeting.

- Be punctual with your meetings—in terms of *your* arrival time—but expect your staff to show up ten to fifteen minutes late. Your Brazilian employees will appreciate the fact that you honor Brazilian time. It is a small concession to make in order to gain commitment from your staff.

- Schedule some meetings in restaurants or clubs for variety, but spread these out.

Participation in Meetings

- Brazilians enjoy sharing their opinions in business meetings. Interruptions are not only tolerated but expected and can come from one's own team members. This is different from the American norm, where interruptions are a sign of rudeness and where one does not interrupt one's teammates.

- Brazilians may talk over one another (talk at the same time) during conversation and may continue to do so until eventually everyone stops talking except for one person.

This practice is also known as "conversational overlap" (see boxed insert, page 38). When a Brazilian is interrupted, it is not necessarily a signal to stop speaking, as it is for Americans. Brazilians tend to continue speaking, sometimes raising their voices over the interrupter in order to be heard. This disregard for taking turns can be very disturbing to a North American.

- The effervescent, spontaneous atmosphere in Brazilian meetings contributes to the problem of maintaining a schedule or sticking to an agenda.

Scheduling Meetings

Many businesses close during Carnival and during important fútbol matches. Be sure not to schedule a meeting during these times.

Participation in Meetings—Suggestions for the Negotiator
- Try not to be exasperated by frequent interruptions from the Brazilian team members. Maintain your focus. This may require that you stop talking and listen, then return to your subject when the interruption ceases, or it may mean that you need to try to talk over your counterpart, which may feel very awkward at first.

Participation in Meetings—Suggestions for the Manager
- Since meetings often go over schedule, all agenda items may not be addressed and a future meeting may need to be scheduled.

- As the conversation becomes more animated, expect to be touched by your Brazilian counterparts (see "Proxemics," pages 38–41).

- Expect your Brazilian employees to share their opinions during meetings, which may be done through interruptions and conversational overlaps.

> *"Brazilians are trained to express their opinions and to argue for them, whether or not they have specific authority behind them."*
> *(Harrison, 26)*

Asking for Agreement

- Asking for agreement requires a long process of negotiation; only after a great deal of time passes does agreement or disagreement eventually surface.

- Brazilians may say yes to a proposal or demand, but this does not necessarily mean agreement; it may mean that they do not want to create discomfort by saying no.

- Brazilians may, on the other hand, say no throughout the negotiation process, but this does not necessarily mean that they do not agree. It may only be an emotional reaction to a perceived obstacle or mean "I/We see it this way" or "We would prefer this to that."

- The collectivist norm of the Brazilian culture makes serious disagreement uncomfortable; Brazilians will want to avoid unpleasantness, such as denying a request or a proposed deal, in order to save face (see "Collectivism," pages 2–4).

Asking for Agreement—Suggestions for the Negotiator
- Continually maintain a friendly atmosphere during the negotiation process; this atmosphere will put your Brazilian counterparts at ease, and they may be more comfortable expressing disagreement.
- Do not take yes as agreement or commitment or no as disagreement. Spend time discussing what you believe the Brazilians are agreeing to or disagreeing with, in order to be sure you understand what is really being said.

Asking for Agreement—Suggestions for the Manager
- In light of what you have already read in terms of power distance (pages 5–7), you might assume that asking for agreement is not something the manager should be concerned with. Definitely do not ask subordinates if they agree with your decision. You may undermine your authority. But remember the dialogue-oriented nature of the Brazilian. Even in situations in which they will, in the end, have no say in a decision, they still want to participate in the dialogue process to let their ideas and feelings be known (and perhaps sway the authority to include their input in the decision-making process).
- For the American manager, asking for agreement does not mean asking for sanction. It means gaining commitment through inclusion. This is accomplished by listening to the Brazilian employee, thereby creating an environment of inclusion, not exclusion (see "Gaining Commitment," pages 66–67).

Dealing with Conflict
- The collectivist norm of Brazilian culture makes conflict something to be avoided. This makes sense in that business colleagues are often relatives or close friends (see "Collectivism," pages 2–4). Offending someone in a work

capacity also may damage relationships with that person in many capacities outside of work.

- Conflict must be dealt with gently and with a view toward salvaging the long-term relationship.

- When conflict does occur, it should be dealt with immediately and privately.

Dealing with Conflict—Suggestions for the Negotiator

- Do not take Brazilian enjoyment of the bargaining process as a sign of conflict. Bargaining and negotiating the details of a project can become effusive and demonstrative, but this is not conflict.

- To ensure that you understand what is really being said (when it is not being said), revisit topics, repeating your team's stance on the subject and asking if team members agree. If you need a direct answer, ask the question, but preface the question with an apology for being direct.

Dealing with Conflict—Suggestions for the Manager

- The best way to deal with conflict between employees is to prevent its occurrence. This is done by keeping open lines of communication between yourself and your employees and keeping abreast of your employees' personal lives (this shows interest and camaraderie).

- Should a conflict occur between employees, address the situation immediately and privately by calling the parties (first individually, then together) into your office or by meeting the parties at a restaurant or club to discuss the problem.

- The American "sandwich technique," in which criticism is offered in stages, much like the layers of a sandwich, may work quite well in Brazil. First, there is acknowledgment of what the employee has done well (one slice of bread), then the negative criticism (the filling), and finally the acknowledgment of the hopes of a continuing good relationship (the second slice of bread). This approach allows the employee to save face.

- The conflicting parties will look to you, the manager, for resolution (remember the paternalistic norm of Brazilian corporate management style). The importance of your responsibility here cannot be overstressed. Even if your style is to let people work out their own disagreements, force yourself to be a mediator.

Managing in a Brazilian Workplace

In managing a workforce in Brazil it is important for you to identify the areas of similarities and differences. The similarities become the pilings for the bridge of communication, and the differences become the springboard for mutual exchange. This section is for the American manager who will be managing a Brazilian or Brazilian/American workforce in Brazil. It identifies some of the similarities and differences between Brazilian and American cultures that will assist American managers in understanding and working with their Brazilian/American workforce. Some of the following material will be a review, or recap, of principles discussed earlier in the manual but expanded upon here.

The differences in corporate cultures (see boxed insert, following page) are a challenge to the American who does not want to waste time building personal relationships with his or her employees. This impatience is often the downfall of the American manager doing business in Brazil.

Differences in Corporate Cultures

Brazil
- Paternalistic
- Authoritarian
- Collectivistic
- Hierarchical
- Employees expect to be taken care of
- Managers expect to be respected by virtue of their position within the organization

United States
- Fraternalistic
- Egalitarian
- Individualistic
- Hierarchy played down
- Employees expect to have to prove their worth
- Managers expect to be respected for their knowledge and ability to lead

Dealing with and Avoiding Problems

- Maintaining face and avoiding embarrassment are of primary importance; consequently, Brazilians will tend to give inaccurate information, such as saying "The subcomponents have been delivered," when only half of the subcomponents were delivered, in order to avoid discomfort. They may also say they understand something when they do not in order to avoid embarrassment.

- Brazilians may be reluctant to take responsibility because they do not want to embarrass themselves by failing. Deal with this by constantly reinforcing them verbally, in writing, and with a reward system.

- Never publicly show impatience or disgust toward your Brazilian employees or colleagues. Such behavior will cause them to lose face, and it will undermine their sense of pride and lead them to respect you less.

- In Brazil, managers use the theory of *jeito* (see boxed insert, below), meaning that they approach the potentially unpleasant project in a roundabout way.

Jeito—"the way around the problem"

Jeito, a Brazilian term that is not directly translatable into English, refers to a way, a skill, or an aptitude. Jeito is an intricate system of giving and receiving favors in order to accomplish a task, and it is used often in business and social relationships. In the words of a foreign businessperson working and living in Brazil, Brazilians are not daunted by obstacles. They simply use jeito to get a job done.

Section Three

Dealing with and Avoiding Problems—Suggestions

- Remember, Brazilians are very demonstrative and punctuate verbal interactions with gestures and other nonverbal behaviors. To the extent that you are comfortable, interact with your Brazilian employees with lots of talking, gesturing, and touching. A quiet demeanor may cause your Brazilian counterparts and employees to feel uncomfortable and unsure of their relationship with you.

- To be certain that your Brazilian employees understand your instruction—and that they have not agreed or said they understood in order to avoid embarrassment—ask them to explain the instruction back to you. But do so carefully and respectfully to avoid loss of face.

- Devise and implement a system that rewards employees for taking responsibilities and risks.

- To be sure that you are obtaining accurate feedback, apply the "trust but verify"[§] system: trust that your employee is providing accurate information, then verify it with your own eyes, or with the assistance of an employee who understands your point of view.

Giving Praise

- Brazilians enjoy praise and positive feedback. It reflects on the individual (remember the high sense of personal pride), the group, and the family. When giving praise, you may do so either in front of a group or privately, and make special note of the consequent contribution to the good of the collective (the department, the company, the organization, etc.).

[§] The concept "trust but verify" is from *Doing Business in Latin America—Brazil*, a video learning program created by Big World, Boulder, CO, 1996.

Giving Praise—Suggestions

- Have a plaque made that lists the accomplishment and names of the team members, and present it during a meeting or office get-together.

- Plan a luncheon or dinner (preferably catered) that includes family members.

- Write a letter to the employee that lists his or her contribution and present it during an office meeting; keep a copy of it in the employee's personal file.

Gaining Commitment: Quality of Life versus Career Success

- Brazilians focus on "quality of life," the emphasis being on relationships and the concern for others. Americans focus on "career success," which rewards assertiveness and the acquisition of money and material things (Adler).

- Focus your management style on the quality of life within the work environment—this means, as we've said so many times before, building strong relationships, socializing, and networking.

- Commitment from your Brazilian employees will come when they feel that you trust and like them. This type of relationship building takes time and energy in the form of not only socializing but also learning about your employees' lives and keeping updated about them.

Gaining Commitment—Suggestions

- Learn what goes on in the office in terms of social interactions—if someone has had an operation, send flowers to his or her home or hospital; if an employee's family member has had a special experience (birthday, scholarship, role in a school play), acknowledge it and ask questions about it.

Section Three

- Make a verbal note when you see an employee going the extra mile on a project.

- Share information about your life, such as a movie or play you recently saw (nothing too intimate though—remember hierarchy and status: the manager is expected to maintain a distance from the rank and file).

Focus and Getting Things Done
- Brazilians focus on the process of a project more than on the end product (the completion); in other words, how a job gets done (emphasis on relationship building) is more important than whether it gets done on time. Americans focus more on the product (the completion of a project). A successful project is one that is completed under or within budget and on schedule.

- One way that Brazilian employees can show their worth to the company is by demonstrating how expediently and efficiently they can expedite the process. This is another example of jeito, the way around the problem. Through jeito, one can recall favors or offer a favor for a promise of return. Because of the endless layers of bureaucracy, especially in the larger cities such as Rio de Janeiro and São Paulo, a person who has the capability to wield jeito is important to the life of the business.

- Successful Brazilian business dealings require ways to deal with bureaucratic red tape. This is accomplished through the use of business contacts and *despachantes*.

> ### Despachante
>
> A *despachante* (dispatcher) is a person who, quite literally, does things with dispatch. Like the business contact, the despachante is important to the success of business negotiations and dealings in Brazil. Such a person has contacts, knows who to speak with, and can get to that person with little difficulty. Without a despachante, bureaucratic red tape will undermine even the most well-planned negotiation or project. Sometimes the despachante is also the business liaison.

- Expect your Brazilian employee to occasionally accomplish tasks through the giving or recalling of favors. Although you may see such actions as illegal, they are not;** they are are simply jeito.

Focus and Getting Things Done—Suggestions

- For most American managers in Brazil, American product orientation versus Brazilian process orientation is one of the most challenging aspects of their job. The best way to appease these conflicting norms is to acknowledge the difference and work with them. Some approaches to this challenge are to

    break processes down into incremental time parameters, then average in additional time for processes to be completed,

---

** Although jeito is usually the exchange of favors, it may be an exchange of money, which may be seen as illegal by authorities of the American company.

Section Three

provide company-sanctioned rewards (see below) for completing steps in the process and getting closer to completing the project, and

continually build relationships with employees to motivate them to want to do a good job for you.

- Maintain regular contact with the home office staff (in the United States) and apprise them of this critical cultural difference. Let them know of your approaches to the challenge.

- From the Brazilian viewpoint, the home office in the United States is viewed as the company's distant grandparent. The more the grandparent is a part of day-to-day operations, the more the Brazilians feel like part of the extended family. Suggest to the home office that it provide a formal list of "company-sanctioned awards," and when these awards are distributed, ask the home office to acknowledge the distribution by a phone call or formal letter to the recipient.

❈ *Section Four* ❈

Protocol

The Art of Eating

General Rules and Information
- Brazilians eat "continental style," using a knife held continuously in the right hand and a fork held in the left.
- Always use the knife to cut food, never the side of the fork. Also, food is cut one piece at a time, then eaten, never cut all at once.
- Always wipe your mouth before drinking.
- While talking, place your silverware on the plate. Do not rest one hand in your lap.
- When a meal is finished, place the utensils parallel (not overlapped) across the far side of the plate (from eleven o'clock to one o'clock if the plate were viewed as a clock).
- The term *jogo Americano* means "American style" and usually refers to an American place setting with a placemat instead of a tablecloth. It may also refer to food being served buffet style.

- At a typical Brazilian meal, the food is served to the plate from platters in the center of the table. Sometimes the host will serve his or her guests, or sometimes the guests will serve themselves. Wait for the host to indicate the protocol by saying either "Please serve yourself" or "Allow me to serve you," in which case you should follow suit.
- Before passing the saltshaker to someone, tap it on the table.
- People do not eat while they walk down the street, except for ice cream or candy. If you buy food at a barzinho, stand near the establishment to eat it.
- Coffee is a beloved drink in Brazil and can be served in a number of ways:

    café com leite (coffee with milk), usually sweetened with sugar

    café preto (black coffee)

    cafezinho (little coffee, usually served in a demitasse cup), sweetened with lots of sugar and no milk

- Coffee is served with the meal for breakfast, but for all other meals, it is served afterward.
- In many businesses, coffee (usually cafezinho) is served every two hours, sometimes with small cakes and cookies.
- Sometimes *matè*, an herbal tea, is served instead of coffee.

Restaurant Protocol

- Never tap a glass or snap your fingers to get a waiter's attention. This is considered very rude. Instead, hold up your index finger and say, "Garçon."

Section Four

- In fast-food restaurants, the bill is usually paid when the food is ordered. In most restaurants, one must ask the waiter for the check. (The Brazilians find the American custom of the waiter leaving the bill on the table insulting, as though the patron will leave without paying.) Request the check by saying *"Conta, por favor"* ("Check please").

- The bill is usually for the entire group. Brazilians find the American custom of requesting separate checks to be rather petty.

- Tipping is acceptable in Brazil. Do not leave the tip on the table, however; either discreetly hand it to the waiter or overpay the bill and leave the restaurant before the change can be delivered. Many restaurants will add a service charge, called *serviço*, to the bill.

Dinner Parties

- If you are invited to someone's home (an honor that should be considered a very special occasion), as the guest of honor, you will probably be seated at the head of the table.

- Dinner parties usually begin late, especially if held at a club or restaurant. Ten or eleven o'clock in the evening is not unusual. The evening may begin with hors d'oeuvres, drinks, and conversation, which may take a great deal of time.

- Americans, used to eating earlier in the evening, may be ravenous by the time food is served, a situation sometimes exacerbated by the fact that alcoholic beverages are usually served before the meal. Many an American has become inebriated during this cocktail hour and embarrassed himself or herself. To alleviate the problem, eat something before you leave for the dinner party.

- If the party is held in someone's home, the host or hostess usually has the meal completely prepared ahead of time. The American custom of the hosts leaving guests to finish preparing the meal is strange to the Brazilians and suggests that the hosts are not prepared for their guests. The meal is usually served by a maid.
- See "Gift Giving," below, for appropriate gifts for the host or hostess.

Typical Meals

- Breakfast usually includes bread and butter, juice, sometimes fruit, and always café com leite.
- Lunch and dinner, the larger meals of the day (some businesses close for a two-hour break for lunch), can include, for example, *arroz e feijão* (rice and beans), *feijoada* (a traditional dish made of beans and meat, traditionally served on Wednesdays and Saturdays), or *farofa* (manioc meal toasted or sautéed in butter and seasonings) served over rice. Fruit and bread are usually included in the meal.
- Water, carbonated beverages, fruit punch, or beer is usually served with meals other than breakfast.

Gift Giving

- Gifts should not be given at the initial business meeting. Wait until the formal meeting is over, then present the gift in an informal situation.
- If you are invited to someone's home, you may bring candy, flowers, or an expensive bottle of wine to the get-together or send flowers the next day (do not include purple flowers). Do not bring food, which suggests that your hosts have not prepared enough dishes for their guests.

- Palm pilots, CD players, inexpensive cameras, name-brand pens, CDs of popular American artists, or liquor are greatly appreciated. Another appropriate gift is granting a favor or buying lunch or dinner.

- Gifts with a predominant color of black or purple, the colors of funerals or death; knives, which symbolize the cutting off of a relationship; or handkerchiefs, which symbolize grief should not be considered as possible gifts.

Styles of Dress

- Brazilians are very fashion conscious. Dressing fashionably is a sign of status, self-respect, and respect for others; poorly or informally dressed individuals give the impression of low self-esteem and low status.

- Styles tend toward the more sophisticated European look as opposed to the more casual North American styles. Colors are muted and well matched. One color combination that usually provokes a good laugh from the Brazilian is green and yellow, the colors of the Brazilian flag.

- Well-manicured hands, cleanly shaven faces, and stylish haircuts are a must for fashion-conscious Brazilians.

- Due to the tropical weather, preferred fabrics are usually natural cottons and silks.

Business Dress

- Upper-management businessmen usually wear three-piece suits; middle-management businessmen, two-piece suits. Men do not wear short-sleeved shirts and usually keep their suit jacket on during meetings.

- Businesswomen wear well-tailored, sophisticated suits and matching accessories.

- Shoes should either match or complement the outfit and should be polished. No sport shoes or sandals are worn by professionals to work. A serious fashion faux pas often committed by Americans is wearing sandals with white socks.

Casual Dress

- Brazilians are very conscious of appropriate dress. At a beach or a club one can expose almost as much skin as one would like (the Brazilian bikini is aptly named "floss"), but one would not wear shorts while walking down the street.

- Usually, only young people (teenagers and younger) wear jeans—clean, pressed, and without holes.

"Almost any appearance in public provides an opportunity to observe and be observed."
(Harrison, 56)

❃ *Section Five* ❃

Information about Brazil

Brazilian History, in Brief

- Prior to 1500, Brazil inhabited exclusively by Indians

1500s

- 1500: Portuguese discovery of Brazil by Pedro Alvares Cabral on April 23, 1500
- 1501: Amerigo Vespucci, sent by King Manuel I, names areas after saints; the land becomes known as *Terra do Brasil*, after a tropical redwood that was its first export; the scarlet dye extracted from it was called *brasa*, meaning "glowing coal"
- 1501–1532: Other European countries move in and raid spice ships
- 1532: Sugar introduced
- 1549: Slave trade begins; first Jesuit missionaries arrive
- late 1500s: War between Portuguese and Dutch settlers

1600s

- 1624: Dutch fleet takes city of Salvador by storm, burning the Jesuit college and killing many priests; the Dutch in turn are attacked by enraged settlers and expelled in 1652 by a combined Spanish and Portuguese fleet

- 1627: the Dutch conquer Olinda and the rich sugar zones of Pernambuco

- 1630: Maurice of Nassau is sent to be the governor of the new Dutch possessions; his enlightened policies allow the Portuguese freedom of religion and include them in the colonial government; during this time, the Dutch West India Company is blamed for the downfall of the Dutch stronghold, because it insists that the Portuguese follow the Dutch practice of Calvinism and be heavily taxed

- 1644: Maurice leaves Brazil in disgust and goes back to Holland; Portuguese settlers rise up against the Dutch and eventually defeat them

1700s

- Guaraní Missions (Spanish and Portuguese Jesuits) flourish

- 1752: Treaty of Madrid divides Brazil between Spain and Portugal, and missions are ordered abandoned; Guaranìs revolt but are defeated by Spanish and Portuguese

1800s

- 1807: Napoleon and his army invade Portugal; the British Navy evacuates King Jõao VI to Rio and declares it the temporary capital of the Portuguese Empire and the seat of the government-in-exile

- 1822: Jõao returns to Portugal and names his son, Dom Pedro, prince regent and governor of Brazil; Dom Pedro

Section Five

declares independence and has himself crowned Dom Pedro I, emperor of Brazil, on 1 December 1822 (Independence Day is now celebrated in Brazil on September 7)

- 1864 to 1870: War with Paraguay (called the War of the Triple Alliance—Brazil, Argentina, and Uruguay)

1900s

- 1901–1930: Immigrants come from Europe and Japan, seeking to make money in the coffee and rubber industries
- 1926: Washington Luis is made president by the elite without an election
- 1930: Revolution led by working-class populist Getùlio Vargas; during this time, the Great Depression hits, dramatically affecting the coffee trade
- 1944: Brazil joins Allies as the Brazilian Expeditionary Force (5,000 strong) and fights in Italy during World War II
- 1945: Eurico Dutra becomes president of Brazil
- 1950: Vargas wins victory for presidency against Dutra
- 1954: Vargas resigns from the presidency under unpleasant circumstances
- 1956–1961: Juscelino Kubitschek (known as "JK") is president
- 1964: Military coup; the new regime lasts twenty-one years and forges the "Economic Miracle" from the mid-1960s to 1974; this combination of high growth and low inflation results in hordes of migrants, who far outnumber available jobs; *favelas* (tenement communities) begin to spread throughout the cities; at the end of this period comes the germination of extreme debt crisis

- 1980s: JK decides to deal with the extreme, crippling debt by opening up and exploiting the Amazon; highway construction begins linking the vast Amazon area to other parts of Brazil; the inhabitants of the Amazon watershed balk at the rapid, unplanned growth and destruction of the area, which results in conflict; international controversy regarding the destruction of the Amazon forest results and continues to rage today

- 1991: Brazilian government liberalizes regulations to facilitate foreign portfolio investments as part of an effort to attract foreign investors

- 1994: Fernando Henrique Cardoso elected president; Cardoso installs *Plano Real* (Real Plan) to stabilize currency

- mid-1990s: *Mercosur–Merado Común del Sur* (the South American Free Trade Agreement) between Brazil, Argentina, Paraguay, Uruguay, and Chile established; Péle, Brazilian fútbol king, is knighted

- 1998: economic crisis; Brazil loses the World Cup to France in the finals

- 1999: Exchange rate of *real* crisis affects all of Latin America; devaluation of the *real* means that the value of the dollar doubles

2000

- preparation begins for new elections

Section Five

Map of Brazil

The Country

The flag of Brazil is green with a large yellow diamond in the center, bearing a blue celestial globe with twenty-seven white, five-pointed stars (one for each state and the Federal District) arranged in the same pattern as the night sky over Brazil. The globe has a white equatorial band with the motto *ORDEM E PROGRESSO* (Order and Progress).

- Conventional long-form name of country in English: Federative Republic of Brazil
- Conventional short-form name of country in English: Brazil
- Long-form name of country in Portuguese: Republica Federativa do Brasil
- Short-form name of country in Portuguese: Brasil
- Capital: Brasília
- Population: over 172 million
- Ethnic divisions: white (Portuguese, German, Italian, Spanish, Polish), 55 percent; mixed white and African, 38 percent; African, 6 percent; other (including Japanese, Arab, Amerindian), 1 percent

- Today there are 250,000 indigenous Indians in Brazil, representing 200 different groups and 180 different languages. They live on 328,185 square miles (equaling 10 percent of the total Brazilian land mass), an area that has been set aside by the federal government so that the Indians may preserve their lifestyle.

Language

Portuguese is the official language; Spanish, English, and French are also spoken.

On the following three pages is a glossary of common Portuguese pleasantries, titles, numbers, and days of the week.

Literacy in Brazil

The literacy rate in Brazil is 83.3 percent (1995 est.). This means that for every one hundred people who apply for a job, seventeen are illiterate. An employee or domestic helper may need to be trained by another employee to do a job because he or she may not be able to read a training manual or a job description.

Pleasantries

English	Portuguese	Pronunciation
Hello	Oi	OH-yee
Good-bye	Tchau (see also page 42)	tchOW (like the Italian *ciao*)
Good morning	Bom dia	bohm Dje-AH
Good afternoon	Boa tarde	boahng
Good evening	Boa noite	boahng NOI-tchee
Sorry	Desculpa	desh KOOL-pah
Excuse me	Com licenca	KOMB lee-SEING-sah
How are you?	Como vai?	KO-moh VI-ee
Fine	Bem	BAMG
Yes	Sim	SEEM
No	Não	NAWNG (nasal tone)
Please	Por favor	POR fah-VOR
Thank you	Obrigado (men)	OH-bree-GAH-doh
	Obrigada (women)	OH-bree-GAH-dah

Section Five

Titles

Mr.	*Sénhor*	sen-HOR
Mrs./Ms.	*Sénhora*	sen-HOR-ah
Doctors and attorneys	*Doctor*	DO-TORH
Professor	*Professor*	PRO-fess-ORH

Numbers

1	*um, uma*	OOM, OOM-ah
2	*dois, duas*	DOI-es, DU-as
3	*três*	TRAY-es
4	*quatro*	KWAH-troew
5	*cinco*	SINK-oh
6	*seis*	SAY-es
7	*sete*	SEH-che
8	*oito*	OI-too
9	*nove*	NOHV-eh
10	*dez*	DAIS
11	*onze*	OON-zeh
12	*doze*	DO-zeh
13	*treze*	TREH-zeh
14	*quatorze*	kwah-TOR-zeh
15	*quinze*	KEEN-zeh
16	*dezesseis*	deh-zeh-SAY-es
17	*dezessete*	DAI-zeh-SEH-che
18	*dezeoito*	DAI-ZOI-to
19	*dezenove*	DEH-zeh-NOHV-eh
20	*vinte*	VEENG-chee
21	*vinte e um*	VEENG-chee-OOM
30	*trinta*	TREEN-tah
40	*quarenta*	kwar-ENH-tah

50	*cinquenta*	seen-KWENH-tah
60	*sessenta*	sehs-SEN-tah
70	*setenta*	seh-TEN-tah
80	*oitenta*	oih-TEN-tah
90	*noventa*	noh-VEN-tah
100	*cem*	SAEM
200	*duzentos*	duh-ZHEN-tos
300	*trezentos*	treh-ZHEN-tos
500	*quinhentos*	keen-HEN-tos
1000	*mil*	MEE-ow (nasal)
2000	*dois mil*	DOI-es mee-ow (nasal)
5000	*cinco mil*	SINK-oh mee-ow (nasal)

Days of the Week

Monday	*segundo-feira*	seh-GUNH-doh FAY-rah
Tuesday	*terça-feira*	TAIR-SUH-ah FAY-rah
Wednesday	*quarta-feira*	KWAR-tah FAY-rah
Thursday	*quinta-feira*	KEEN-tah FAY-rah
Friday	*sexta-feira*	SAIS-tah FAY-rah
Saturday	*sàbado*	SAH-BAH-doh
Sunday	*domingo*	doh-MING-goh

Government

- Type of government: federal republic
- Administrative divisions: 26 states and one federal district (*distrito federal*), Brasília: Acre, Alagos, Amapà, Amazonas, Bahía, Ceará, Distrito Federal, Espìrito Santos, Goiàs, Maranhão, Mato Grosso, Mato Grosso do Sul, Minas Gerais, Parà, Paraìba, Paranà, Pernambuco, Piauì, Rio de

Janeiro, Rio Grande do Norte, Rio Grande do Sul, Rondonia, Roraima, Santa Catarina, São Paulo, Sergipe, Tocantins

- Branches of government

    Legislature:
    - National Congress
    - Two houses
        Chamber of Deputies
        Federal Senate

    Executive:
    - Headed by President of Republic

    Judicial:
    - Federal Superior Court
    - Superior Court of Justice
    - Regional courts
    - Specific courts

- American Embassy in Brazil: SES-Av. das Nações, Quadra 8d, Lote 03, 70403-900-Brasília, D.F.; phone: 061-321-7272; fax: 061-225-9136; hours 8:00 A.M.–5:00 P.M. Monday through Friday.

Holidays

- Easter Sunday

- Carnival, a five-day festival preceding Ash Wednesday

- Tiradentes Day (April 21) celebrates the death of Joaquim José da Silva Xavier, a dentist and nationalist known as Tiradentes, who died in the struggle for independence

- Labor Day, May 1

- *Fiesta Junina* (June festivals) coincide with the feasts of Saint John and Saint Peter, celebrated with local fairs

- Independence Day, September 7 (from Portugal in 1822)
- Memorial Day, November 2
- Republic Day, November 15
- Christmas Day (Christmas Eve is the day of the big meal, usually turkey or ham, and when gifts are exchanged; gifts from Santa Claus are found on Christmas Day)
- New Year's Eve (*Candomblé*, an Afro-Brazilian religion, also honors the sea goddess *Iemanjá* at this time; people dress in white and blue to honor her and to get energy for the new year)

Economy

- Brazil has South America's largest GDP
- Industries: textiles, shoes, chemicals, cement, lumber, iron ore, tin, steel, aircraft, motor vehicles and parts, other machinery and equipment
- Currency: 1 real (R$)=100 centavos

Communications

- Communications systems in Brazil are modern and reliable, with e-mail, fax, and Internet services available.

The Amazon

- The Amazon extends for 6.5 million square kilometers, of which 3.5 million square kilometers are in Brazil.
- It contains, at any given moment, more than one-fifth of the world's fresh water.
- There are an estimated 15,000 animal and insect species in the Amazon, thousands of which have not yet been identified, and untold numbers of unclassified plants.

- Hundreds of acres of the Amazon forest are being destroyed daily for the production of rubber, cattle ranching, paper mills, timber mills, mining, and other uses. Although these industries have created jobs and opportunities for Brazilians, these focuses are slowly changing.

- The Brazilian government and private sectors are realizing that the products of this vast area provide sustainable growth potential without destroying the forest. Some examples are the fruits, roots, nuts, and medicinal plants contained in the forest, which are useful to pharmaceutical companies. There is also a growing interest in ecotourism, which brings money into the region without exploiting the natural environment.

Race in Brazilian Culture

The Brazilian culture is known for what has been called "racial democracy." People of different cultural backgrounds seem to coexist successfully. Indeed, if one were to read most books on the subject, one might believe that the Brazilian culture has established what the American culture has only dreamed about—the perfect melting pot. When we look deeper at the social structure of Brazil, however, we find certain facts that do not support this melting pot image. For instance, the average income for white Brazilians is twice that of black Brazilians (Cleary, Jenkins, Marshall, and Hine 1994). Demographic studies show that blacks, mulattos (the offspring of blacks and whites), and Indians have lower degrees of education than does the white population—a factor that continues to hold these three groups at the lower rungs of the socioeconomic ladder.

Still, when looking at the melting pot ideal, in which people of different cultural backgrounds can interact as a healthy unit, the Brazilian culture can be considered the most successful culture thus far.

Foreign negotiators will more often be negotiating with white Brazilians because whites have more access to higher education and the opportunities that it offers. Even so, management and staff in Brazilian offices will likely include a broad cross section of cultural backgrounds.

The American managing a Brazilian workforce will rarely find the degree of social unrest that can exist in the United States, where people from different cultural backgrounds may refuse to work with each other or may exhibit obvious antisocial behavior. The Brazilian employees are more inclined to get along. This is due, in part, to the collectivistic and very social nature of the Brazilian culture (see Sections One and Two for information about Brazilian social and cultural values).

Bibliography

Adler, Nancy J., ed. 1997. *International Dimensions of Organizational Behavior.* Cincinnati: South-Western College Publishing.

Axtel, Roger E. 1991. *Gestures—The Do's and Taboos of Body Language around the World.* New York: John Wiley and Sons.

Cleary, David, Dilwyn Jenkins, Oliver Marshall, and Jim Hine. 1994. *Brazil, the Rough Guide.* London: Rough Guides Ltd.

Hall, Edward T. 1983. *The Dance of Life.* New York: Anchor Books/Doubleday.

———. 1981. *Beyond Culture.* New York: Anchor Books/Doubleday.

Hall, Edward T., and Mildred Reed Hall. 1990. *Understanding Cultural Differences: Germans, French and Americans.* Yarmouth, ME: Intercultural Press.

Harrison, Phyllis A. 1983. *Behaving Brazilian: A Comparison of Brazilian and North American Social Behavior.* Cambridge, MA: Newbury House.

Hofstede, Geert. 1980. "Motivation, Leadership, and Organization." In *Organizational Dynamics* 16, no. 4.

Leaptrott, Nan. 1996. *Rules of the Game—Global Business Protocol*. Cincinnati: Thomson Executive Press.

Lewis, Richard D. 1999. 2d ed. *When Cultures Collide—Managing Successfully across Cultures*. London: Nicholas Brealey.

Morrison, Terri, Wayne A. Conaway, and George A. Borden. 1994. *Kiss, Bow or Shake Hands*. Holbrook, MA: Adams Media.

Rocha, Jan. 1997. *Brazil in Focus: A Guide to the People, Politics and Culture*. New York: Interlink Books.

Training Management Corporation. 1995. *Doing Business Internationally...The Cross-cultural Challenges*. New Jersey: Princeton Training Press.